THE
ULTIMATE KID'S GUIDE TO WEATHER

BY JENNY MARDER

GROSSET & DUNLAP

GROSSET & DUNLAP
An imprint of Penguin Random House LLC, New York

First published in the United States of America by Grosset & Dunlap,
an imprint of Penguin Random House LLC, New York, 2024

Visit us online at penguinrandomhouse.com.

Library of Congress Cataloging-in-Publication Data is available.

Manufactured in China

ISBN 9780593658949

10 9 8 7 6 5 4 3 2 1 TOPL

Design by Taylor Abatiell and Abby Dening

CONTENTS

THE HURRICANE HUNTERS

Off the coast of Africa over the Atlantic Ocean, a storm is taking shape. As it moves west toward the United States, it grows bigger and more powerful. Its winds pick up speed and spiral around a center, like a spinning top. It is on its way to becoming a hurricane—the most violent type of storm on Earth.

In Mississippi, five brave workers board an airplane, and begin to fly toward the growing storm. They are the Hurricane Hunters. Their mission is to fly straight into the eye of a hurricane, measure the storm from the inside, and send back valuable information. As they get close, the plane starts to shake.

It is a dangerous job. So much can go wrong when flying into a wildly spinning storm. Wind could damage one of the plane's wings or its landing gear or knock out an entire engine. The plane could get struck by lightning. But the team has trained for all of it.

The airplane enters the storm. The shaking gets stronger. Each hurricane has its own personality. This one is like an old wooden

The **GOES-16 satellite** captured this image of Hurricane Ian approaching Florida on September 27, 2022. GOES-16 keeps a fixed watch over most of North, South, and Central America, collecting data on severe storms and other weather events.

roller coaster, and it is making the plane jerk up and down and side to side.

Master Sergeant Karen P. Moore is the loadmaster. She has an important job: to drop instruments called **dropsondes** out the bottom of the airplane.

She moves to the center of the plane, bracing against the shaking. Another team member, the weather officer, calls out, "Load. Release the sonde." Moore opens a large tube and slides the dropsonde inside. Then she presses a button, and the instrument shoots out from the bottom of the plane. "Sonde away!" she says.

The dropsonde, which is attached to a parachute, falls through the storm. As it falls, it measures the speed (and direction) of the wind, the storm's temperature, the pressure of the surrounding air, and how much water the air contains. It sends the measurements back to Moore in the airplane in real time.

Master Sergeant Moore watches a screen. She is looking for four lines of data, a sign that it's a "good drop."

Lockheed Martin Aeronautics

Master Sergeant Karen P. Moore is a loadmaster/ dropsonde operator for the 53rd Weather Reconnaissance Squadron at the Keesler Air Force Base in Mississippi.

Within twenty minutes, the National Hurricane Center will receive these measurements and send them on to weather forecasters, who will report the storm on television and on the radio. Governors will use the data to send warnings: "Get to higher ground," these warnings will say. "Evacuate."

This data will save lives.

The plane flies in and out of the hurricane for hours, and Moore drops about thirty dropsondes—enough to measure and map the entire storm.

Days later and ten thousand feet below, when the storm finally arrives at the coast, the winds will whip, and the waves will crash into the shore. Wind from a hurricane can knock over trees and destroy buildings. Water can surge from the sea onto land, causing deadly flooding.

But because of the work done by the Hurricane Hunters, people won't be surprised. They'll have boarded up windows to protect their homes. They'll have escaped to emergency shelters or fled the area.

In this book, you'll learn about the complicated dance of wind and water and air and temperature that makes up the weather. You'll learn about storms so dangerous they flatten buildings and blow away cows. You'll learn about weather events so bizarre they baffle scientists. You'll learn about the difference between weather and climate, and what you need to know about how our climate is changing.

CHAPTER ONE

WHAT IS WEATHER, ANYWAY?

The weather has a reputation as the most boring of conversations. The sun shines, the rain falls, the wind blows, the seasons change. Yawn, right?

Wrong! It's anything but boring. Earth's weather does crazy things. A tornado can fling an 18-wheeler truck in the air and strip the feathers off a chicken. The coldest weather can freeze your eyelashes; the hottest can bake cookies on the dashboard of a car.

In this chapter, we give you the tools to wow your parents and friends with your weather forecasting skills.

A tornado races across the ground near Dodge City, Kansas, 2016.

Ryan McGinnis/Moment/Getty Images

A man takes a selfie in snow.

The Atmosphere

All weather happens in the **atmosphere**, the area of gases that surrounds our planet.

In 2014, a man named Alan Eustace rode a giant balloon more than twenty-five miles into the sky, and then was cut loose, plummeting to Earth. He was dressed in a space suit and attached to a parachute. His goal: to set the record for the highest human free fall—and solve some tricky engineering problems while doing it.

Sound Smart

The atmosphere gives us the oxygen we breathe, keeps us warm, and protects us from harmful radiation from space.

7

Alan hung facing the ground as the balloon carried him into the sky. As he rose into the air, the world below him got smaller. At first, he saw pebbles on the ground, and then people and cars, and then cities, and then states. For two hours, the balloon carried him up.

The atmosphere is divided into five layers, like layers of a cake. The bottom layer of the Earth's atmosphere is the troposphere. The **troposphere** is where we live and where most planes fly. This is also where weather happens. Above that is the **stratosphere**, which protects us from ultraviolet radiation from the sun. There are three other layers even higher called the mesosphere, thermosphere, and exosphere.

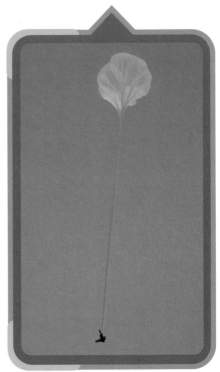

Alan Eustace is lifted into the stratosphere by a balloon.

Dave Jourdan

Alan rose through the troposphere and into the stratosphere, where he saw thin, lacy clouds. Few humans have spent any time in the stratosphere because it's so high, higher than most planes fly. In the stratosphere, the oxygen was so thin and the temperature so cold that Alan needed a special space suit that pumped oxygen and heat. The space suit also connected him by radio to his support team on the ground.

At his highest point, Alan was surrounded by the blackness of space. He described it as "ink black." He could see the curve of the Earth below him. He had a moment of wonder, of appreciating the beauty of his home planet. And then he began to fall.

As Alan fell, he backflipped twice and then steadied

himself with his elbows to avoid spinning dangerously out of control. He flew faster than the speed of sound, triggering a sonic boom that could be heard on the ground, and reached 822 miles per hour at his fastest speed. After four minutes and twenty-seven seconds of free fall—just imagine falling for that long—he opened his parachute and crash-landed on the ground in New Mexico. It was, at the time, the highest skydive ever recorded.

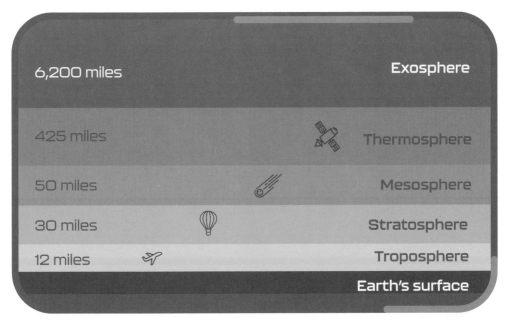

6,200 miles	Exosphere
425 miles	Thermosphere
50 miles	Mesosphere
30 miles	Stratosphere
12 miles	Troposphere
	Earth's surface

Numbers are approximations

After falling to Earth from the edge of space, Alan's crew removed his helmet, and a doctor said, "How do you feel?" Alan laughed. "Good," he said. "But tired."

Reading a Weather Map

Scientists who study the atmosphere to understand and predict the weather are called **meteorologists**. Meteorologists tell us if it's sunny or rainy or snowy or windy, so we know what to wear and how to plan our day. More importantly, they tell us if dangerous weather is headed our way, like a tornado, a hurricane, or a blizzard, so we can take shelter or evacuate to safety.

To do their job, meteorologists need to know about all sorts of things, but especially these five: **temperature**, **wind**, **water vapor**, **precipitation**, and **air pressure**.

Weather Pop Quiz

Do you know which is which? Draw a line to the answer.

1. *TEMPERATURE*

2. *WIND SPEED AND DIRECTION*

3. *WATER VAPOR*

4. *PRECIPITATION*

5. *AIR PRESSURE*

A. The weight of air

B. How hot or cold something is

C. Liquid water or ice that forms in the atmosphere and falls toward the Earth's surface

D. A gas in the atmosphere. It is needed for clouds, rain, and snow

E. How fast air moves from one place to the next, and which way it's moving

ANSWER KEY: 1B, 2E, 3D, 4C, 5A

Meteorologists use measurements of these things to make **weather maps**. And then they use the weather maps to do two main things:

1. report the weather happening now, and
2. predict, or forecast, future weather.

Let's look at these five weather conditions a little closer.

TEMPERATURE: How hot or cold something is. Meteorologists pay close attention to thirty-two degrees Fahrenheit, the point at which water freezes.

Hot air rises and cold air sinks. And this is important for every aspect of weather. As you'll see, this rising and sinking drives rain, thunderstorms, and wind.

REMEMBER THIS: Hot air rises, cold air sinks.

Try This at Home:
Cricket Thermometer

You can (sometimes) tell the temperature by counting a cricket's chirps. Male crickets chirp by rubbing their front wings together, and they chirp faster when it's warmer, slower when it's cold.

Here's how you do it: Set a timer for fifteen seconds. Count the number of chirps during that time. Add forty. That should be the temperature, or close to it, in Fahrenheit.

For example, say you counted thirty chirps in fifteen seconds. Add forty to that number. The temperature is seventy degrees Fahrenheit.

Now this isn't foolproof. It won't always work. That's because a cricket's chirp can change according to its age or how hungry it is. Also, crickets don't usually chirp at very hot or very cold temperatures. But try it, and then check the temperature outside. How close did you get?

A brown cricket crawls on the ground.

WATER VAPOR: We all know that water can be liquid or solid, right? There's liquid water that we drink and frozen water, or ice. Water vapor is when water is in its third state: a gas.

You know the steam that rises from a hot shower or makes a teapot whistle? Or the puff of air that you breathe out of your mouth on a cold day? That mist you see comes from tiny water droplets suspended in the air. When they disappear, they become water vapor. Water vapor is needed for clouds and the things that come from clouds, like rain and snow.

PRECIPITATION: Rain and snow are both types of precipitation. So are sleet, hail, and freezing rain. Nearly all precipitation comes from clouds. And clouds are made when water vapor turns into liquid or ice.

People walk in the rain with umbrellas on a Halloween night.

AIR PRESSURE: Air pressure, or atmospheric pressure, is the weight of the atmosphere above and around you, and that weight changes depending on the weather. In fact, most weather comes from air trying to move from high pressure to low pressure. The greater the difference in pressure, the faster the air moves.

Air pressure can tell you a lot about what kind of weather to expect. When air pressure is high, that means molecules are crowded together, and the air is sinking because of the weight. A **high pressure system** usually means the weather is sunny and mild.

REMEMBER THIS: Air moves from high to low pressure.

When air pressure is low, molecules have more space to move around, and as the air rises, the temperature cools and clouds form. That's why a **low pressure system** often means weather that's cloudy or stormy or rainy.

REMEMBER THIS: A high pressure system often means weather that's sunny and mild. A low pressure system often means weather that's cloudy or stormy.

DiD YOU KNOW?

At sea level, air typically weighs 14.7 pounds per square inch. That means every inch of your head is holding the weight of a heavy bowling ball. Air pressure is all around us, pushing us from all sides. But you don't get crushed by that weight, or even feel it, because the weight of air is distributed over a large surface and the fluid in your body pushes outward with the same pressure as the air.

Try This at Home:
Air Pressure Experiment

1. Fill up a cup or glass one-third full of water

2. Cover the mouth of the cup with an index card.
   (The index card must cover the entire opening.)

3. At the sink, turn the cup and index card upside down.
   (Hold the index card in place as you do this.)

4. Remove your hand.

WHAT HAPPENS? The index card should stay in place. This is because the water weighs less than the air below. Nearly fifteen pounds of air is pushing up on the index card, compared to less than a pound of water pushing down. Cool, right?!

WIND SPEED AND DIRECTION: Wind speed is how fast air moves from one place to the next. Wind direction is where it's going. Wind blows from areas of high pressure to low pressure.

People struggle to walk against wind and rain.

It All Works Together

These five things—temperature, air pressure, water vapor, precipitation, and wind—don't work alone. They're always working together to create weather conditions.

How we feel temperature, for example, is influenced by both wind and moisture. Hot temperatures feel hotter to us when there is more moisture in the air. The measurement of the amount of moisture in the air is called **humidity**. If you've been in Washington, DC, or Florida or Texas on a hot summer day, you know what humidity feels like.

Sound Smart

The combination of air temperature and humidity is called the **heat index**.

The air feels sticky and heavy. And it can make a big difference in the temperature. A temperature of 95 degrees Fahrenheit with humidity of 50 percent *feels like* 107 degrees.

And when you add wind to cold temperatures, the temperature feels even colder. That's called **wind chill**. A temperature of 40 degrees Fahrenheit combined with a wind speed of 20 miles per hour *feels like* 30 degrees.

gjohnstonphoto/
iStock/Getty Images

A boy sweats after practice.

Try This at Home: Use a Sponge to Illustrate the Amount of Moisture in the Atmosphere.

A sponge full of water is at 100 percent relative humidity. It's so wet the sponge can't hold anymore, and the water drips out, like rain from a cloud. A sponge half full of water is at 50 percent relative humidity. A sponge with no water? You guessed it: zero humidity.

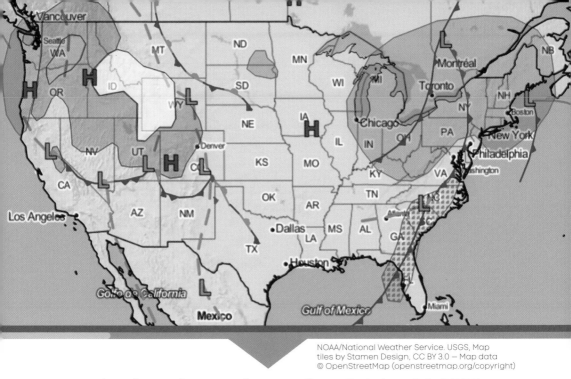

A National Weather Service map from October 24, 2022

Introducing . . . the Weather Map!

Meteorologists rely on weather maps to study the weather. Take a look at this weather map above. Each color and symbol has an important role.

In a weather map, blue lines always mean cold air, and red lines always mean warm air. The *H* means an area of **high pressure**. The *L* means an area of **low pressure.** Remember, high pressure means crowded air molecules, sinking air, and clear, often sunny weather. Low pressure means air molecules rising up to form clouds, so cloudy or stormy weather.

The red and blue lines on the weather map represent a **weather front**. That means simply, the front, or edge of warm or cold air. A blue line shows a front of cold air. A red line is, you got it, a front of warm air. These are called **cold fronts** and **warm fronts**.

The triangles on the blue lines point to the direction the cold air is moving. The semicircles on the red lines point to the direction the warm air is moving.

When weather fronts are present, weather changes. This could look like dramatic thunderstorms, rain, gusty winds, tornadoes, or a drop in temperature.

Watch the Weather

Take note of the wind's direction. Strong winds from the south mean a cold front is approaching. You can tell when the cold front has passed by watching trees, flags, or smokestacks. The winds flip direction as the front moves through.

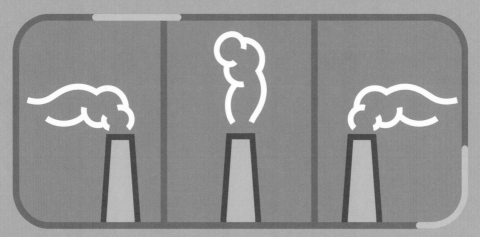

You'll learn more about weather maps as you go through this book. And the next time you want to know whether you should wear sneakers or rain boots or if your soccer game will be canceled, don't check an app or wait for others to tell you.

Instead, go to the National Weather Service's Weather Prediction Center (www.wpc.ncep.noaa.gov). Pull up a weather map and try to predict the weather yourself. Are there high pressure conditions in your neighborhood? It's likely a clear day for your soccer game. See a weather front in your area? You might be playing in the rain.

You'll know soon enough if you got it right!

CHAPTER TWO

THE WEATHER OUTSIDE

Consider this. The glass of water you drank today could be made of the same molecules that rained on your great-grandparents' home one hundred years ago. That's because the amount of water on Earth never changes.

Water is a shape-shifter, moving around our planet, rising up and falling down, and changing form as it does so. And it's a good thing we have so much water, because it's needed by all life on Earth.

Massimo Ravera/ Moment/Getty Images

A rainforest on a rainy day

22

The Water Cycle

In an incredible process that's powered by our sun, water is constantly being exchanged between atmosphere, ocean, and land.

Ice, or frozen water, is found in glaciers and snow. Water vapor is found in the atmosphere. And **liquid water** is found in oceans, lakes, and rivers.

It works like this: The sun shines onto ice and snow, warming it and making it melt into liquid water that streams into oceans, lakes, and rivers. Heat from the sun also causes liquid water to **evaporate**, becoming water vapor in the

Sound Smart

Nearly **97 percent of water on Earth is salty ocean water. Another 2 percent is in the planet's glaciers and ice caps. That leaves just 1 percent for drinking water and other water needs.**

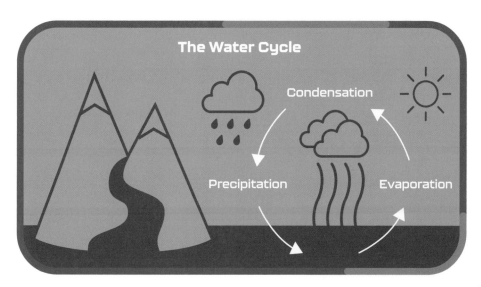

The Water Cycle

Condensation

Precipitation

Evaporation

A road with trees in Dresden, Germany,
seen throughout the seasons

atmosphere. That water vapor goes up, up, up into the atmosphere until the cool air turns it into liquid water or ice, in the form of a cloud. This is called **condensation**. And then it falls back down as rain or snow. That's precipitation.

The Earth and the Sun and the Seasons

Of course, how hot or cold it is outside depends in large part on the season. We all know that days are longer and warmer in summer and shorter and cooler in winter. But why does the weather change throughout the year?

Don't know? Don't worry, you're not alone. In fact, you'd be surprised how many people can't answer this question. It's been estimated that more than 95 percent of people—including college students—get it wrong when asked.

You're about to become the other 5 percent.

To understand the seasons, you need to know about a few things: the Earth's equator, the Earth's poles, and how our planet orbits and spins.

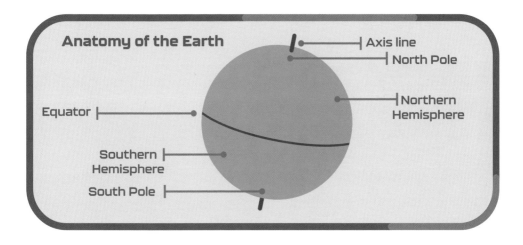

Anatomy of the Earth

Axis line

North Pole

Northern Hemisphere

Equator

Southern Hemisphere

South Pole

The very top and very bottom of the Earth are called the **North Pole** and **South Pole**. Now imagine an imaginary line around the middle of the Earth, like the black line of a Pokémon ball that splits the red upper half from the white lower half. That imaginary line around Earth is called the **equator**, and it splits the Earth into two equal parts. Everything above the equator is the **Northern Hemisphere**. Everything below is the **Southern Hemisphere**.

Imagine another line that runs through the middle of the Earth from the North to the South poles, as if you just poked a giant toothpick through the planet. That line is called the **axis**.

Sound Smart

From one birthday to the next, you've made one full trip around the sun.

The Earth spins on its axis like a top. One full spin, or **rotation**, takes twenty-four hours—one day. If you're on the side of the Earth facing away from the sun as it spins, that's night. If you're on the side facing the sun, that's day.

Fuse/Corbis/ Getty Images

A teacup ride at the fair

DiD YOU KNOW?

The sun rises and sets faster at the equator than anywhere else on Earth. It takes about 20 minutes there to go from day to night.

As the Earth spins on its axis, it is also going around the sun. So it spins at the same time as it orbits. Think about a teacup ride at a theme park that spins as it moves in a circular motion. That's what our planet is doing. One trip around the sun, or **orbit**, takes the Earth 365 days, or one year.

Here's where we get to the seasons. Take a look at this picture. The Earth doesn't spin straight up and down on its axis. It's always a little bit tilted. And voilà, your answer!

This tilt is why it's cold in winter and hot in summer.

You can see in this picture how Earth's axis always points the same direction, but because of the tilt,

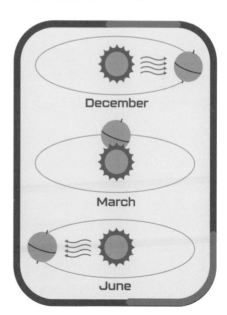

December

March

June

the sun's rays hit the Northern Hemisphere for more hours of the day one time of year, and the Southern Hemisphere for more of the day another time of year. When the Northern Hemisphere is tilted toward the sun, that's summer in the Northern Hemisphere and winter in the Southern Hemisphere. So summer in the United States happens at the same time as winter in Australia. When the Southern Hemisphere is tilted toward the sun, the seasons switch. In September and March, the sun shines equally on both hemispheres.

Longer daylight hours give the Earth plenty of time to reach those hot summer temperatures.

Changing Weather

Here's a look at different kinds of weather you'll find throughout the seasons.

Cloudy Weather

The atmosphere is a fluid, which means it moves and flows like water in a river. Because the atmosphere is made up of invisible gases instead of liquid, we rarely get to see this. But clouds are our window into the

Clouds moving over the Earth as seen from space

UFO-shaped clouds are called lenticular clouds. This one is passing over Mount Lassen in Lassen Volcanic National Park.

movement of the atmosphere! Watch the clouds for a few minutes, or take a time-lapse video of them, and you'll see it yourself.

There are so many different kinds of clouds. Some are scary, some are beautiful, some are downright bizarre. Some look like giant cotton balls packed together, some like cauliflower, some like waves.

Clouds that look like cotton balls are called altocumulus clouds.

Remember, evaporation happens when the sun heats the water in lakes and oceans and makes water particles rise upward as water vapor. As those particles get higher and the atmosphere gets colder, they condense into clouds.

Our atmosphere needs to be a little dirty for this condensation to occur. This is because in order for water droplets to form, the water vapor must first wrap itself around a tiny piece of dust, dirt, smoke, or—over the ocean—salt. The water forms, or condenses, around that particle, eventually becoming a water drop or ice cystral.

Clouds are simply a collection of tiny water droplets or ice crystals floating in the sky. The way a cloud looks and how it behaves comes from different combinations of wind, air temperature, and air pressure.

For this experiment, you'll need a clear water bottle, water, and matches.

1. Add water until the bottle is three-quarters full.
2. Close the bottle and shake it.
3. Now, light a match, open the bottle, and drop the match in.
4. Squeeze the bottle and you'll see a cloud forming.

WHAT CAUSES THE CLOUDS? Shaking the bottle adds water vapor to the air space, and the flame adds smoke. Water is able to wrap around the smoke particles, forming tiny water vapor droplets. In other words, clouds!

DiD YOU KNOW?

Clouds often look light and fluffy, but all that water weight adds up. A typical cloud weighs more than a million pounds. That's as much as fifty large school buses.

WATCH THE WEATHER

Wispy **cirrus** clouds like this often mean a storm system is coming.

Puffy, white **cumulus** clouds like this usually appear on fair days. However, grayer cumulus clouds, like stratocumulus clouds, or growing cumulus clouds that appear early in the day usually signal afternoon or evening thunderstorms. A cloud that's as tall as it is wide is another thing to watch for. That probably means rain is on the way.

skhoward/iStock/
Getty Images

Wispy cirrus clouds in a blue sky

Gray cumulus clouds that appear early in the day often signal afternoon or evening thunderstorms.

Steve Proehl/The Image Bank/Getty Images

There's an old saying: "A ring around the sun or moon means rain or snow is coming soon." These rings come from light that reflects off water particles in the atmosphere and scatters. But while they sometimes correspond with rain, they're not the best weather predictor.

A ring around the sun seen from the Po Valley, Italy

Wet Weather

Water droplets inside clouds grow by colliding with other droplets and combining to eventually form a raindrop. Bigger raindrops eat smaller ones and grow. Rain happens when the drops get so big and heavy that the cloud can't hold them anymore and they spill out. Remember the sponge dripping with water?

DiD YOU KNOW?

Raindrops are often drawn in the shape of teardrops, but they're shaped more like jelly beans or tiny hamburgers.

The record for the rainiest place on Earth goes to the village of Mawsynram in India. The village gets more than 450 inches of rain each year. People who live there wear a special kind of full-body umbrella made of bamboo and banana leaf called a knup.

Lightning and Thunder

Rain is sometimes, but not always, accompanied by **lightning**, a giant spark of electricity in the atmosphere. The temperature of the air where there's lightning can get as high as fifty thousand degrees Fahrenheit. That's five times hotter than the surface of the sun!

Thunder is simply the sound that lightning makes, and because light travels faster than sound, you see the lightning before you hear the thunder.

Don't mess with lightning. About twenty-eight people in the United States die each year from lightning strikes. And most of the people who die from lightning are outdoors.

You're most at risk if you are outdoors, next to something tall like a tree or a light pole or near water.

DiD YOU KNOW?

You can tell how far away lightning is by counting the seconds between the flash of lightning and the sound of thunder. It takes the sound of thunder five seconds to travel one mile. So count the number of seconds between the lightning and thunder and then divide by five.

- ◼ twenty seconds = four miles away
- ◼ five seconds = one mile away
- ◼ zero seconds = zero miles away!

Stay Safe in a Lightning Storm

- ☐ Stay away from elevated areas like hilltops or roofs. Lightning strikes the highest point.

- ☐ Get out of swimming pools, lakes, or other bodies of water.

- ☐ Get indoors if you can.

- ☐ If you can't, get into a car with a hard top.

- ☐ If you're away from a home or car, go to a low-lying area, and stay away from tall objects like trees.

- ☐ Avoid taking a shower or a bath or washing dishes during a thunderstorm. It's unusual, but lightning can travel through plumbing and shock people.

⋜ Sound Smart ⋞

Astronomers study lightning on other planets by listening to the radio waves the lightning flashes emit.

You can listen to lightning on Earth, too, using a dead AM radio station in your car. If you're close enough, you'll find lightning's radio waves sound like bacon sizzling and popping in a hot pan.

Meindert van der Haven/iStock/Getty Images

Lightning flashes during a thunderstorm.

World Record!
Longest Lightning

The world's longest recorded lightning flash stretched 477 miles, from the central coast of Texas and across the state of Louisiana, all the way to southern Mississippi.

The National Oceanic and Atmospheric Administration's (NOAA) Geostationary Operational Environmental Satellite-16, also known as GOES-16, measured what is believed to be the longest lightning flash on record on April 29, 2020.

NOAA

WILD WEATHER: In a place called Lake Maracaibo in Venezuela, lightning strikes three hundred days of the year, often many times a day.

Thunderstorms

The surface of the Earth, whether it's land or ocean or forest or ice, absorbs heat from the sun. Remember, hot air rises and cold air sinks. Thunderstorms start with a mass of warm, humid air rising from the surface and colliding with cold air. Warm ocean water, for example, evaporates into lots of moisture. As the air rises, the pressure drops and the air cools, making water droplets form, and with them, clouds. The more warm air rises, the bigger the cloud.

When the water droplets get heavy enough, they fall as rain or hail, and a powerful rush of cold air falls with them. That cold air hits the ground, spreads out, and forces warm air to rise ahead of it. This rising and falling air happening at the same time is called a **convection cell**.

A **summer thunderstorm** in Bulgaria

John Sirlin/EyeEm/
Getty Images

A supercell thunderstorm **near St. Francis, Kansas**

The most powerful and long lasting of these storms are called **supercells**. Hot air fuels these storms, and in the strongest thunderstorms, air rises as fast as one hundred miles per hour. Most tornadoes come from supercells.

There are two ingredients that you typically see in thunderstorms that become supercells:

Sound Smart

Rising air is called an **updraft.** Descending air is called a **downdraft.**

1. Moisture, or warm, humid air in the lower levels of the atmosphere.
2. A fast flowing current of air higher up called a **jet stream**, which produces something called **wind shear**. Wind shear is wind that changes its speed or direction as it gets higher.

READ A WEATHER MAP

The green and dotted green regions in the map below indicate rain and thunderstorms. See how they often correspond with a low pressure system, and where cold and warm fronts meet? Look at the key at the bottom left to see what the other colors represent.

Weather map from the morning of December 10, 2022

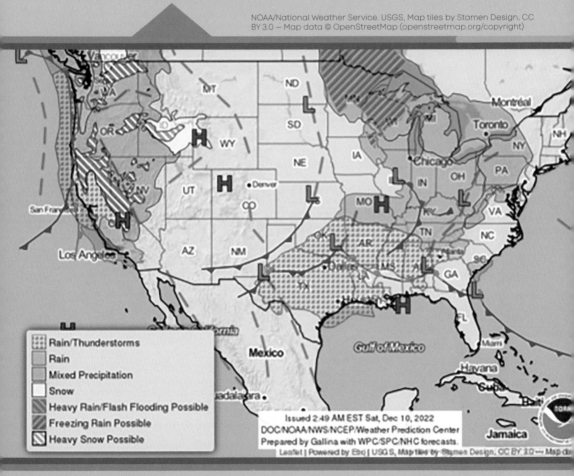

Key:
- Rain/Thunderstorms
- Rain
- Mixed Precipitation
- Snow
- Heavy Rain/Flash Flooding Possible
- Freezing Rain Possible
- Heavy Snow Possible

Issued 2:49 AM EST Sat, Dec 10, 2022
DOC/NOAA/NWS/NCEP/Weather Prediction Center
Prepared by Gallina with WPC/SPC/NHC forecasts.
Leaflet | Powered by Esri | USGS, Map tiles by Stamen Design, CC BY 3.0 — Map da

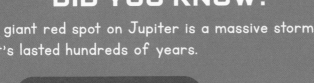

DiD YOU KNOW?

The giant red spot on Jupiter is a massive storm that's lasted hundreds of years.

The Hubble Space Telescope captured this image of planet Jupiter and its red spot.

NASA/ESA/Goddard/ UCBerkeley/JPL-Caltech/ STScI

Snowy Weather

Have you ever looked at a snowflake under a microscope? Take a look at the photo. Dazzling, right?

Snowflakes, just like raindrops, are born when water droplets in clouds freeze around dust particles, but in this case, instead of forming water drops, they create tiny **ice crystals**.

ChaoticMind75/iStock/ Getty Images

A microscopic look at a snowflake

41

Because of the shape of water molecules, they freeze into a pattern with six sides. And if conditions are right and temperatures are low enough, the ice crystals stick to other ice crystals, growing arms, and branches, and more branches.

Sleet and Freezing Rain

Did you know that snow, sleet, and freezing rain all start out as snow? The difference has to do with the temperature of the air that they fall through.

If the temperature stays below freezing all the way from the cloud to the ground, you'll have **snow** on the ground. **Sleet**, those gunky, slushy raindrops, occur when the snow falls through a warm layer of air and a freezing layer below that, melting and

Freezing rain coated this branch with ice.

then freezing. **Freezing rain** happens when the snow melts completely while falling and then freezes as it hits the ground, tree branches, power lines—whatever it comes in contact with—creating a layer of ice.

Wild Weather

Freezing rain makes a car look like a glazed donut and can make branches and power lines so heavy that they snap.

Freezing rain creates a glazed-donut effect on a car.
CatEyePerspective/iStock/ Getty Images

Hail

Hail forms inside big, dark thunderclouds, the same clouds that cause thunder and lightning. Heat makes water particles rise high up into the sky and wind blows these droplets even higher, where it's so cold that the water drops freeze into ice. They get heavy and

Hail **lies on the grass after a hailstorm.**

fall, and then wind blows them up again, where they collect more water that freezes into ice. This keeps happening until they get too heavy to be blown up by the wind and fall to the ground.

Most hailstones are pea-size, but some are the size of golf balls or even bigger.

Record: Largest Hailstone

The largest recorded hailstone fell in South Dakota in 2010. It was eight inches in diameter. That's about the size of a volleyball!

Windy Weather

Wind is just air moving around our planet. It is a super complicated system, but it all comes down to these three simple things:

1. The Earth is warmer at the equator.
2. The Earth is colder at the poles.
3. The Earth spins.

Since the sun shines directly over the equator and at an angle to the poles, the ground at the equator gets hotter than it does at the poles. If the Earth wasn't tilted and if it didn't spin, air circulation would be simple. That hot air would rise into the upper atmosphere and then spread out, moving north and south toward the poles, where it would sink as it cools and travel back to the equator. It would look something like the graphic above.

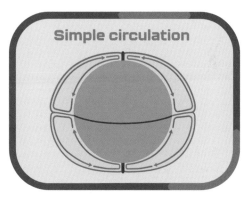

Simple circulation

But because the Earth rotates, the Earth is tilted on its axis, and there's more land than water in the Northern Hemisphere, it's all much more complicated. It actually looks like the graphic to the right, with three different circulation patterns instead of one big one.

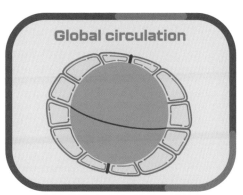

Global circulation

Different Types of Wind

TRADE WINDS blow east to west just north and south of the equator, carrying ships west across the Atlantic from Europe or Africa to North or South America. Trade winds steer hurricanes.

WESTERLIES blow west to east between the midlatitudes between the Tropic of Cancer and the Arctic Circle in the north and the Tropic of Capricorn and the Antarctic Circle in the south.

JET STREAMS are rivers of fast-moving air that blow much higher in the upper troposphere. They flow five to nine miles above the Earth's surface. In the United States, they mostly travel from west to east. But sometimes they meander like a river, also shifting north or south. And, importantly, they are like the highways of a storm, carrying weather systems with them and controlling where storms go.

LOCAL WIND: Local geography can affect wind, too. Mountains, lakes, and oceans can all create wind. For example, it tends to be windy by oceans and lakes. This is because land heats up faster than water during the day, causing a **sea breeze** that blows from the ocean onto the shore. Over the ocean, there are also no buildings, trees, or hills to block the wind.

Sound Smart

A plane trip from Los Angeles to New York is much faster than a New York to Los Angeles flight. This is because airplanes fly in jet streams, and the wind speeds up their flight time.

46

READ A WEATHER MAP

The dark red lines in the map are called **isobars**. They represent changes in pressure. The closer together the lines are, the higher the wind speed.

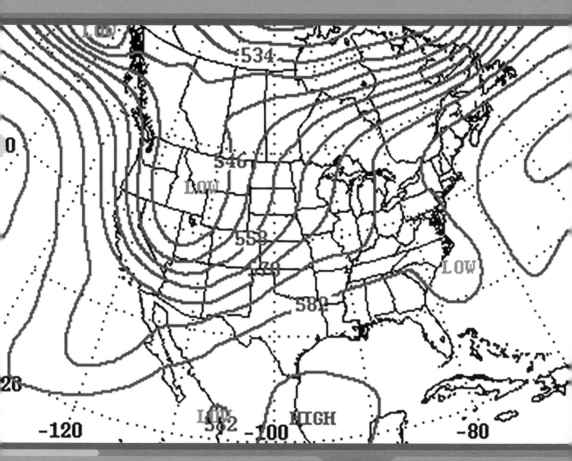

National Centers for Environmental Prediction, Weather Prediction Center/NOAA

Isobars on this surface weather map from October 23, 2022, show changes in air pressure.

Global Weather Patterns

When it comes to weather, everything on Earth is connected. Weaker trade winds can mean warmer ocean waters. A warmer Pacific Ocean shifts the US jet stream south, influencing weather changes all over the world: floods and landslides in some areas and drought and heat waves in others.

When the surface of the ocean in the central and eastern Pacific gets warmer than usual, that's called **El Niño** and when it gets cooler, it's called **La Niña**.

El Niño can mean torrential rain and heavy snow in the southwestern United States and

NASA/Goddard's Scientific Visualization Studio

The dark blue area in the center of this image shows cool sea surface temperatures along the equator during a La Niña episode.

unusual heat in Brazil. La Niña can mean cooler, wetter weather in the Pacific Northwest and stronger Atlantic hurricanes. And there are more effects worldwide. Fish thriving in one area of the ocean and dying in another. Flowers bursting into bloom in a barren desert in Chile.

For example, it might look like the photo on the next page. As trade winds slow, water in the Pacific Ocean warms. Warm water rises into water vapor, fueling rainfall in South America. All that rainfall makes desert flowers bloom in an explosion of color.

**Flowers bloom in the Atacama Desert
in Chile after unusual rain.**

Congratulations! You now know more about weather than most adults. But what about when the weather takes a turn for the worse? Read on.

CHAPTER THREE

DANGEROUS WEATHER

Tornadoes

It was evening in southern Kansas, and the sky had turned a dark greenish color. Outside it was eerily quiet. The day had been hot and windy, and a supercell thunderstorm had moved into the area. A whirlpool of air hung from the cloud, suspended like a swirling snake. Then it touched the ground, and the silence was replaced by a roaring sound, like a freight train. Inside a rotating thundercloud, a massive tornado had formed—a monster. And it was heading straight toward a town called Greensburg.

Emergency sirens rang through the town. "Your time is up," the meteorologist said on the local television news. "You need to be in your shelter *right now*."

The tornado moved over the Kansas farmland, swirling and hopping across the ground. And then it entered the town. As it barreled through, it pulled trees from their roots, tore apart homes, and crushed cars. It flipped trucks and sheared buildings from their foundation.

The tornado that struck Greensburg on May 4, 2007, was nearly two miles across, as wide as the town itself. It was believed to have wind speeds greater than

Metal siding wraps around a tree stripped bare of branches and leaves by a tornado in Greensburg, Kansas, in May 2007.

Cultura RM Exclusive/Jason Persoff Stormdoctor/ Image Source/Getty Images

A **tornado** near Dodge City, Kansas, on May 24, 2016.

two hundred miles per hour. By the time it passed through, eleven people had died, and nearly all of the town's homes and buildings had been destroyed.

Fortunately, most of Greensburg's 1,500 residents survived. Some listened to the warnings and fled the town. Many escaped to basements or tornado shelters. Some pulled mattresses over their bodies as their houses fell down around them.

A **tornado**, a violently rotating column of air that extends from a thunderstorm cloud and touches the ground, is one of nature's most violent storms. It's also one of the most mysterious.

What Makes a Tornado a Tornado?

A rotating cloud is not considered a tornado until it touches the ground.

⇉ Sound Smart ⇇

Kansas sits in Tornado Alley, an area of the United States that stretches from South Dakota to Texas, where tornadoes are most likely to occur. This is because of the combination of warm, humid air rising from the Gulf of Mexico combined with the jet stream, which delivers cold fronts and storms.

WIND GUST SPEED (MILES PER HOUR):

In 2007, meteorologists introduced a new scale to rate the intensity of tornadoes.

RATING	3-SECOND WIND GUST (MPH)	DAMAGE
EF0	65–85	Minor
EF1	86–110	Moderate
EF2	111–135	Strong
EF3	136–165	Severe
EF4	166–200	Devastating
EF5	Over 200	Incredible

You know how water swirls when going down a drain? A tornado is like that, too, but it's made of wind instead of water, and, like a vacuum, that wind sucks air into the storm as it swirls. Inside a thundercloud, where warm and cold air meet, changing wind direction and wind speed create a horizontal spin, like a rolling pin. As the spinning air is drawn into the rising air, or **updraft**, of the thunderstorm, that horizontal spin tilts up into a vertical wind funnel.

Tornado winds are the strongest winds in the world. But the biggest danger—the cause of most injuries and deaths—comes from objects and debris that are picked up by the storm and sent flying.

Record:
Widest Tornado

The widest recorded tornado struck El Reno, Oklahoma, in 2013. It was 2.6 miles wide.

That's What We Know.
Here's What We Don't Know:

Scientists are still learning more about how tornadoes form. And it's not always clear why some storms produce tornadoes when other storms in similar environments don't.

Hurricanes

From space, a hurricane looks like a rotating coil of clouds organized in a beautiful spiral pattern. But on the ground, it feels like heavy rain and fierce, terrifying winds. These winds can reach two hundred miles per hour.

Like tornadoes, hurricane winds can snap trees, knock down homes, and destroy whole communities. But hurricanes are bigger than tornadoes and last longer. And while tornadoes form over land, hurricanes form over the ocean.

The deadliest part of a hurricane is the floodwater it brings. Hurricane floods occur when heavy rain and winds push huge amounts of ocean water

An overturned car and damaged home in Gulfport, Mississippi, in the wake of Hurricane Katrina

MichaelWarrenPix/iStock Unreleased/Getty Images

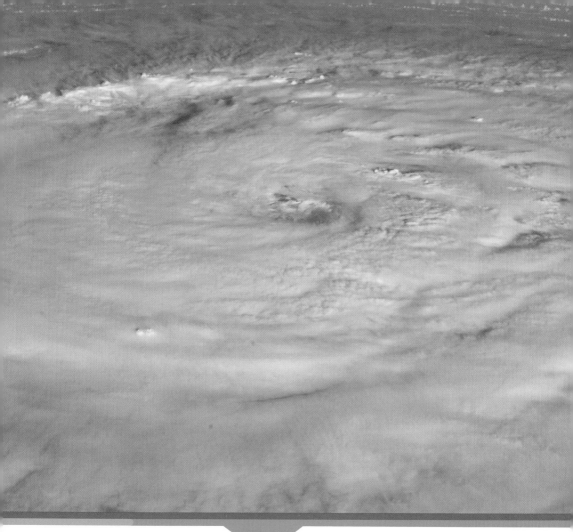

A view of Hurricane Larry is seen from the International Space Station.

onto land. This is called a **storm surge**. As a result of Hurricane Katrina, which struck Louisiana and Mississippi in 2005, more than 1,800 people died, most because of storm surge flooding.

Hurricanes in the United States usually form over the Atlantic Ocean or the Gulf of Mexico, though the ones that impact Hawaii form over the Pacific Ocean. They begin as tropical storms and are fueled by moist air and warm ocean water, the way wood fuels a fire.

What Makes a Hurricane a Hurricane?

When wind speeds reach seventy-four miles per hour, a tropical storm becomes a hurricane.

Hurricanes have a unique structure. A hurricane's **eye** is its clear center and the calmest part of the storm. The eye typically stretches from twenty to forty miles across. It is surrounded by a **wall** of deep clouds and deadly winds. At the outer edge are **rainbands**, lines of heavy rain and thunderstorms that spiral toward the storm's center. When a hurricane is passing over, heavy rain and powerful winds can suddenly give way to clear skies as the eye is overhead, and then start all over again with the other side of the hurricane.

Spiral rainbands

Hurricane eye

Cameron, LA

Eye wall

GOES-16/NOAA

A satellite image of Hurricane Laura, Louisiana coastline, August 27, 2020

THE SAFFIR-SIMPSON HURRICANE WIND SCALE

This scale rates hurricanes based on their wind speed and estimates possible damage.

CATEGORY 1
**Winds 74 to 95 mph.
Even the weakest hurricane-force winds are dangerous and will cause some damage.**

CATEGORY 2
**Winds 96 to 110 mph.
Increasingly dangerous winds will cause major damage.**

CATEGORY 3
**Winds 111 to 129 mph.
Extensive damage can be caused by these devastating winds.**

CATEGORY 4
**Winds 130 to 156 mph.
Severe damage to structures and the surrounding area will occur at these high wind speeds.**

CATEGORY 5
**Winds 157 mph or higher.
These extreme winds produce catastrophic destruction and widespread damage.**

Storms with the most well-defined eyes are often the strongest. For example, see in the image from page 57 the nearly perfect circular eye of Hurricane Laura, which made landfall in Louisiana in August 2020 as a Category 4 storm. The storm's 150-mile-per-hour winds knocked over trees and power lines, blew windows out from high-rise buildings, and sheared the top off a walking bridge.

Fortunately, with forecasting tools, scientists can predict when a hurricane is coming, usually several days in advance.

see in the image from page 57

Sound Smart

Hurricanes are called different things in different parts of the world. Over the northwestern Pacific Ocean and Asia, they're called typhoons. In the Southern Hemisphere and Indian Ocean, they're called cyclones. In the United States, they're called hurricanes.

DID YOU KNOW?

Each Atlantic Ocean hurricane gets a name. They are named in alphabetical order, and the first storm each year starts with A. Some letters aren't included though: Q, U, X, Y, and Z. Also, names get retired after the worst storms. We'll never again have a Hurricane Katrina or Sandy or Andrew.

STAY SAFE IN A HURRICANE

- Have an evacuation plan. Know where the nearest emergency shelters are and make sure the car has gas or is charged. Follow news alerts and do what they say.

- Evacuate if you are in an area at risk of a storm surge or flooding.

- Have an emergency kit ready. It should include bottled water, canned food, batteries, flashlights, a battery-operated radio, and a first aid kit.

- If you have not been ordered to evacuate, stay inside when the hurricane hits. Secure outer and inner doors.

- Shelter in a room without windows, or in a closet.

Blizzards

When a snowstorm gets windy and wild, it can sometimes become a blizzard. Remember weather fronts? Blizzards happen when cold and warm air meet. And they can drop *lots* of snow.

WILD WEATHER: February 2015 was an unusually snowy winter in Boston; the city got more than seven feet of snow in three weeks. For fun, people were jumping off high windows and balconies onto snow-covered streets below. It was really dangerous, and eventually the mayor had to make a safety speech. "Stop this nonsense," he said.

Blizzards don't only come from falling snow, they come from snow blowing around so much they make the world look white. Think howling winds, freezing temperatures, and so much blowing snow that you can barely see where the ground meets the sky. Blizzards make travel dangerous and block roads.

Cars in downtown Manhattan were covered in snow after a **severe winter storm** the night before.

belterz/E+/Getty Images

During a blizzard, it's not unusual for power to go out and travel to become impossible, sometimes for several days, which can make it difficult to get medical care.

Blizzards need enough cold temperatures and enough moisture in the air to form the crystals in clouds that make snowflakes. That moist air and cold air meet in a weather front and the warm air rises above the cold air. Many blizzards form from **Nor'easters**, a type of storm that travels up the East Coast of the United States with winds from the Northeast.

Two big dangers in a blizzard are **frostbite** and **hypothermia**. Hypothermia happens when the body temperature drops too low. This can make a person lose the ability to think clearly. Frostbite is an injury from freezing and usually affects the fingers, toes, ears, cheeks, or chin.

What Makes a Blizzard a Blizzard?

A snowstorm has to meet the following three criteria to become a blizzard: thirty-five mile per hour winds, low **visibility**, and it has to last at least three hours.

gremlin/iStock/Getty Images

STAY SAFE IN A BLIZZARD

If a person is showing signs of frostbite or hypothermia:

- ☐ Seek medical help as soon as you can.
- ☐ Get them into a warm room or shelter.
- ☐ Remove wet clothes.
- ☐ Warm them with dry clothes and blankets.
- ☐ Place areas affected by frostbite in warm water.
- ☐ Don't walk on feet or toes with frostbite and don't rub or massage frostbitten areas.

Heat Waves

A heat wave is a period of unusually hot weather usually lasting more than two days.

During the worst heat waves, roads buckle, train tracks warp, and asphalt can burn skin. While heat waves may be less exciting than tornadoes or lightning storms, they are often deadlier. In fact, heat waves cause more deaths than any other weather event.

This is because high temperatures can put you at risk of heat exhaustion or heatstroke. Our bodies need to be able to keep cool. Remember that air temperature plus humidity is called heat index? Well, the heat index in the worst heat waves can be over

A boy walks over a dry lake bed.

one hundred degrees and is often worse in buildings without air conditioning. This is higher than our normal body temperature, which means our bodies have to work harder to stay cool.

In high heat, it's important to drink lots of water and stay cool. If your friends ever seem confused in the heat, tell an adult right away—confusion is often a sign of heatstroke.

A **heat dome** occurs when the atmosphere traps hot ocean air like a lid on a pot that holds steam and heat inside. This comes from high-pressure air sinking down. A heat wave in the Pacific Northwest in 2021 killed hundreds of people, many of whom were home alone with no air conditioning.

STAY SAFE IN A HEAT WAVE:

- ■ Drink lots of water.
- ■ Dress cool.
- ■ Find shade.
- ■ If you don't have air conditioning, find an air-conditioned place to cool off, like a library or cooling center.
- ■ If you need to do strenuous activity, drink water and take frequent breaks.
- ■ Avoid being in a parked car with the windows closed.
- ■ Cool off in sprinklers, a pool, a cool bathtub, or with an ice pack.

Drought

Drought is caused by lack of rain or snow over a period of time. Remember that the *H* on a weather map means high pressure, resulting in clear conditions and sunny weather. During a period of drought, it's as if that *H* has dropped anchor like a boat and is locked in place over an area. That can mean too much sun, and not enough rain, making an area too dry.

Plants die because the soil is not getting enough moisture. Lakes, rivers, and reservoirs can shrink or dry up. And dry temperatures and wind can make it easier for wildfires to ignite and spread.

DiD YOU KNOW?

You can see drought in tree rings. The number of tree rings tells you how old the tree is. The thickness tells you how much it rained that year. Wider rings mean more water. Thin rings mean the water was scarce.

But that's not all. Here are some other weather events:

DUST STORMS: Dust storms occur when wind lifts large amounts of sand or dust into the atmosphere. In northern Africa, strong winds from the Sahara Desert carry sand and dust off the coast and over the Atlantic Ocean to North and South America. This mass of dusty air can reach twenty thousand feet high into the atmosphere and travel several thousand miles, grounding flights and turning the sky orange. Intense dust storms are called **haboobs**. Dust storms also occur in the southwestern United States.

ICE STORMS: A storm that produces huge amounts of ice because of freezing rain. Ice can weigh down trees and power lines, causing them to collapse. It can also make roads and bridges dangerous for people and cars.

MONSOONS: A monsoon is a shift in winds that happens when the seasons change. It can cause a very rainy or a very dry season and is known for occurring in Asia near the Indian Ocean, though it can occur in other places, like the southwestern United States.

ATMOSPHERIC RIVERS: An atmospheric river is a narrow storm system that moves tremendous amounts of water vapor through the atmosphere. They can be responsible for extreme amounts of rain, snow, and flooding.

FIRE TORNADOES: Sometimes smoke and heat from wildfires create their own extreme weather. They form clouds that produce lightning, rain, wind, and even, rarely, fire tornadoes.

Chapter Four

PREDICTING THE WEATHER

O n September 8, 1900, a powerful Category 4 hurricane slammed into the seaside city of Galveston, Texas. The winds reached 135 miles per hour, and the storm pushed water onto land. The water rose fast until it was fifteen feet above normal levels—that's nearly the height of a two-story house—and rushed through the city. Within hours, the wind and water had destroyed a hospital, a schoolhouse, and three thousand homes. More than eight thousand people died that day. It was one of the worst disasters in the history of the United States.

The aftermath of the hurricane in Galveston, Texas, in 1900

George Grantham Bain Collection/
Library of Congress

The weather forecast from the September 8, 1900, edition of the Galveston Daily News read "Rain Saturday with high northerly winds."

You can't stop a hurricane, but you can warn people that it's coming so they have time to get to safety. The reason so many people died that day in Galveston is they had no warning. The weather forecast in the city's daily newspaper simply predicted rain and high winds. And that forecast was buried on page 8.

Never again will a storm like this arrive with no warning. That's because meteorologists now have special tools that allow them to watch the weather and predict what the weather will do next. Most of these tools didn't exist at the time of the Galveston storm.

Consider the things meteorologists study to understand the weather, like temperature, air pressure, wind, and water vapor. Those measurements are captured by **space satellites**, **ocean buoys**, **weather balloons**, **radar**, and observations on the ground.

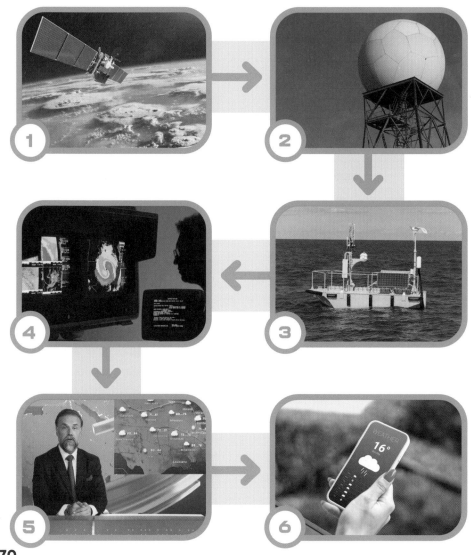

Weather Forecasting Pop Quiz

Do you know which is which? Draw a line to the answer.

1. *WEATHER SATELLITE*

A. An instrument that floats or drifts in the ocean, collecting data

2. *RADAR*

B. A machine or group of machines that can do calculations thousands or a million times faster than a personal computer

3. *OCEAN BUOY*

C. This carries an instrument high in the air that measures temperature, pressure, and moisture

4. *WEATHER BALLOON*

D. An instrument that sends pulses of energy into the atmosphere to measure rain or snow

5. *SUPERCOMPUTERS*

E. A spacecraft that circles the Earth and tells us things about the weather

Weather Satellites

Imagine traveling the distance between Washington, DC, and Detroit, but up. There, circling our planet, is a weather satellite the size of a rhinoceros that measures water vapor and temperature all over the atmosphere. Think of it like sticking a giant thermometer into the sky.

Weather satellites are our eyes in the sky. They are loaded with high-tech instruments and launched by rockets into space. In space, they zip around our planet, snapping pictures of Earth and measuring all kinds of weather events. These weather satellites are why we will never again be surprised by a hurricane like the people were in Galveston back in 1900.

Weather satellites have gotten much better over the years. This was the image from the very first weather satellite that launched in 1960. It's the first satellite image we saw from space. That fuzzy white stuff on the planet? Those are clouds.

Now compare that to what satellite images look like in 2022. The image on page 73 taken by a weather satellite shows Hurricane Dorian making landfall in North Carolina in September 2019. Can you see the hurricane's spiral pattern in the clouds?

NASA

The first image captured by the TIROS I satellite on April 1, 1960

This image of Hurricane Dorian was taken by a geostationary satellite on September 6, 2019.

There are two kinds of weather satellites.
Polar orbiters circle the Earth from the North Pole to the South Pole, as the Earth spins underneath. These satellites measure

many different things: hurricanes and wildfires, dust storms and volcanoes, polar ice and heat waves, and the health of the ocean.

It's amazing if you think about it. All the way from space, satellites can accurately measure the temperature of the surface of the ocean. They can also measure the insides of a hurricane, as if taking an X-ray of a storm from space. They can tell you the temperature and amount of water vapor in different parts of the storm.

As much as 85 percent of the data that goes into a weather forecast comes from polar-orbiting satellites.

This helps scientists predict what path the hurricane will take and how strong it will become.

Geostationary satellites are much farther away from Earth than polar orbiters, and they orbit at the same rate the Earth spins. What this means is that each satellite keeps a constant watch on a giant section of the planet. This way, they see a hurricane or a tornado or a dust storm in motion. They measure lightning strikes. They detect wildfires and watch them grow. All of this helps meteorologists develop warnings for people on the ground.

These satellites also measure weather in space, such as giant bursts of energy from the sun that can send waves of radiation toward Earth. This radiation can be harmful to power grids on Earth and to astronauts in space.

Doppler Radar

Meteorologists use radar to measure rain and snow and to determine the severity of thunderstorms. There are more than 150 radar towers across the United States. These towers send out pulses of energy and then record the amount of that pulse that has bounced off rain, snow, and other particles in the atmosphere. This is similar to the way bats or whales use something called echolocation to bounce sound off things to know what's around them.

Computers analyze the amount of time the radio pulses take to travel there and back, and their strength. The strength tells you about the size and shape of the object. The time tells you about its distance.

Sound Smart

Scientists use radar in space, too. Radar from a spacecraft helped them map the surface of planet Venus.

NASA/JPL/USGS

This image of the surface of planet Venus was created with observations from more than a decade of radar imaging.

READING A WEATHER MAP

The image below shows what radar looks like on a weather map. This kind of map is often included in weather apps. The map below is from August 10, 2020, the day a powerful derecho blew across the central United States, causing wind damage, downed trees, flattened crop fields and power outages. A **derecho** is a fast-moving, destructive line of thunderstorms. Remember, radar measures precipitation. Green on this map means light rain. Yellow means a medium amount of rain. And red means a lot of rain. It can also mean hail. A radar map also tells you what direction clouds and rain are moving so you know if weather is headed your way.

Des Moines Radar/National Weather Service/NOAA

Weather Balloons

Every day, all over the planet, scientists release giant balloons filled with hydrogen or helium that float up into the atmosphere, expanding as they rise. These balloons start at about the length of a lion and expand to the size of a medium U-Haul truck. The biggest can expand to the size of a football field.

Attached to the bottom of the balloons are **radiosondes**. Remember the dropsondes that hurricane hunters drop from planes? Radiosondes are similar, but in this case, they go up into the stratosphere instead of dropping down to Earth. The balloons rise and rise and rise. And when they reach about one hundred thousand feet, they pop and float back to the surface. As they rise, the balloons measure temperature, pressure, and humidity, and beam these measurements back to scientists on the ground.

milehightraveler/iStock/Getty Images

Ocean Buoys

Buoys are floating objects placed throughout the ocean that capture important ocean data. The data might be used by a ship captain choosing to reroute a ship around stormy seas. It helps in search and rescue operations if a boat is missing. And it gives climate scientists critical information to better understand how the oceans are impacted by climate change.

Surface Observations

There are about nine hundred weather stations across the United States that take weather measurements every few minutes of wind, precipitation, air pressure, and visibility in the sky. Thousands of human volunteers also train to become "storm spotters" or to track and report weather conditions like rain or snowfall rate or river levels in their area to the National Weather Service.

Supercomputers

All of this data goes into some of the world's most powerful computers. Two new computers recently joined the fleet of supercomputers at the National Weather Service. These computers are so special and powerful that they have their own names: Cactus and Dogwood.

Supercomputers like Cactus and Dogwood take this enormous amount of data from all the instruments mentioned above—radar, satellites, weather balloons, and ocean buoys—and make unimaginably fast calculations.

The calculations are fed into **weather models**. And these weather models are like very powerful computer programs that use math to make predictions. In other words, these computers help meteorologists model and predict the weather. The supercomputers produce a **global weather forecast**, four times a day. And it's all the basis for . . . you guessed it, weather maps.

Sound Smart

Cactus and Dogwood operate at the power of twelve petaflops. Think of it this way. If you wanted to operate at just one petaflop, you'd have to do one calculation every single second for your entire life, and then for an additional thirty-one million years. A one petaflop supercomputer could do all those calculations in one second.

CHAPTER FIVE

CLIMATE CHANGE IS MAKING WEATHER WORSE

O n the morning of August 20, 2018, a fifteen-year-old girl named Greta Thunberg sat down alone on the cobblestones outside the Swedish parliament. Beside her was a backpack and a water bottle. In front of her, one hundred flyers that she'd made and placed under a rock containing climate change facts. And leaning against the wall was a sign she'd painted that said, "School Strike for Climate." Instead of going to school that day, she had ridden her bike to the government building to protest for more action on **climate change**.

It had been a summer of fierce heat waves and massive wildfires in Sweden. For several hours, Greta sat outside the government building by herself. But eventually, others began to sit with her. And then more and more. She kept protesting, and by November of that year, she had inspired more than seventeen thousand students in twenty-four countries to strike for climate change. By March, that number had reached two million and Greta was being invited to give speeches all over Europe.

"Our house is on fire," she told a roomful of world leaders in Switzerland. "I am here to say our house is on fire."

Weather and Climate

Think about our Earth. Our beautiful planet with apple trees and waterfalls and eagles and lizards and lightning bugs.

You've heard that climate change is hurting our planet. But what exactly does it mean?

To understand climate change, you first need to understand the difference between climate and weather.

The **weather** is what's happening right now, outside your window. It might be sunny and warm or drizzly and cold. And that might suddenly change as clouds come in or the rain clears.

NASA

This view of the Earth was captured by the Apollo 17 crew on its way to the moon on December 17, 1972.

Meanwhile, the **climate** is the patterns of weather over a longer period of time. Say you live in Virginia. You probably know to expect hot, sticky weather in the summer, and chilly days with a chance of snow in the winter.

Another way to think of it is that weather is like your mood, which can change many times in a day. You might feel happy or curious or frustrated or disappointed, and how you're feeling probably makes you act a certain way. Climate is more like your personality. It's the pattern of your moods and behaviors over a longer period of time. A person might be described as having a cheerful or fiery or funny personality. Of course, a generally cheerful person has moments where they feel sad. An outgoing person has moments of feeling shy.

Science fiction writer Robert Heinlein once aptly described it this way: "Climate is what you expect, weather is what you get."

The Climate Is Changing

The climate has changed lots of times over Earth's long history, freezing and then warming again. But this time, it's different. That's because this time, humans are causing the change.

You've probably heard that the Earth has been getting hotter. Since 1880, the world's average temperature has increased by about 2 degrees Fahrenheit. And most of this warming has occurred since 1975. The world is warming, and that warming is happening faster.

But it's not just the temperature. Weather all over our planet is also getting more unpredictable and more extreme.

How did we get here? Look around your home. The ceiling lights, the television, the video game system, the toaster; all of these things are powered by electricity.

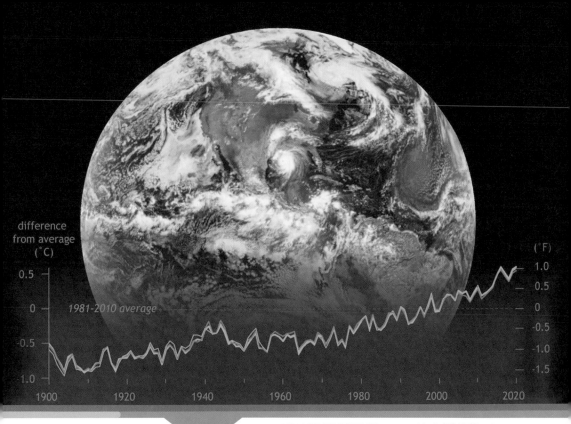

NOAA DISCOVR/EPIC/Climate.gov Media/NOAA Climate.gov

Data from NOAA (red line), University of East Anglia (pink line), and NASA (orange line) all show that Earth's average temperature has been warming from 1981 to 2020.

⋛ Sound Smart ⋚

The terms *global warming* and *climate change* are often used interchangeably, but they mean different things. **Global warming** describes the rising of Earth's global temperature. Climate change describes the changes in climate caused by global warming. For example, rising sea levels; melting ice at the North and South poles; and more intense storms, heat waves, and wildfires.

Most of our electricity is delivered through power lines that run along our street and connect to power stations. Many of these power stations create electricity by burning something called **fossil fuels**.

Think about how you get places. Do you take cars, buses, trains? Fossil fuels power most vehicles. They also provide heat.

Fossil fuels are made from dead animals and plants that lived hundreds of millions of years ago. When they died, they sank to the bottom of oceans and swamps. Deep inside the Earth, heat and pressure cooked these dead plants and animals to create a black, sticky liquid called **oil** and a special kind of gas called **natural gas**. Ancient trees and plants hardened over many millions of years to make **coal**.

Greenhouse Gases

Getting these fossil fuels out of the ground and burning them to create electricity releases **greenhouse gases** like **carbon dioxide** and **methane** into the air. These gases released into the atmosphere are called **emissions**.

Imagine a greenhouse with sunflowers and tomatoes and cucumbers growing inside. The glass traps heat from the sun inside the greenhouse, keeping the flowers and vegetables warm, even when it's cold outside. In the atmosphere, the way that greenhouse gases trap heat is called the **greenhouse effect**, because the gases act like a blanket, making our planet warm just like the greenhouse keeps plants warm.

A certain amount of greenhouse gases are needed on Earth. They keep our planet warm enough for life to exist. But it's a

Greenhouse in a garden

delicate balance. Too many greenhouse gases trap too much heat, which raises Earth's temperature too much, too fast. That's what's happening now.

MEET THE GREENHOUSE GASES

- ■ Carbon dioxide
- ■ Methane
- ■ Nitrous oxide
- ■ Hydrochlorofluorocarbons
- ■ Water vapor
- ■ Ozone

Here's a Look at Some Other Ways That Greenhouse Gases Are Released:

→ Most cars, trucks, and planes are powered by burning fuel.

→ Cars vent exhaust from their tail pipes.

→ Power stations pump out pollution.

Trees are like sponges that take in and store carbon dioxide. When trees are burned or decompose, that stored carbon dioxide gets released into the air. And it's a double whammy when forests are cut down, because not only do the trees eventually release their stored carbon, but they also aren't around anymore to pull carbon dioxide out of the air.

Methane is released when cows burp and fart. Cows burp a lot because gases are created when their stomachs break down grass. And these emissions, especially burping, are responsible for a huge amount of global greenhouse gas emissions. Methane is also released when frozen soil in the Arctic thaws and organic waste trapped underneath decays, and from the mining, transport, and production of fossil fuels.

Fluorinated gases are used to cool refrigerators, freezers, buildings, and cars. These can stay in the atmosphere for *thousands* of years.

Rising Seas, Shrinking Ice

This is what climate change looks like. Hot weather is getting hotter. Mountain glaciers and ice at the poles are melting. This melting makes ocean water levels rise. Meanwhile, warmer waters make the ocean expand. Rising and expanding oceans means more flooding along the coasts. Droughts and heat waves are getting worse in many places. Wildfire seasons are getting longer.

In some areas, climate change might mean more snow or stronger hurricanes or rainstorms.

Cherry, peach, and apple trees are especially sensitive to changing weather. Because of warmer-than-normal temperatures, the trees get confused, bloom too early and then get killed by a spring freeze. That can put an end to the orchard for the year.

Flooding and drought damages farms and makes it hard for people in some areas to access food and water.

Changing weather also makes it harder for animals to find places to live. Carbon dioxide sinks into the oceans, making the ocean water more acidic, which means death for many shellfish and coral, which disrupts the food chain for other sea animals.

Two Americas, Two Worlds

In our country and all over the world, climate change is hurting poor communities the most.

Consider a heat wave. A week of one-hundred-degree days is different if you don't have air conditioning in your home. A hurricane headed for your town is more dangerous if you don't have a car and can't easily get to safety. A bad growing season for crops is devastating for farmers with no other source of income.

A cruel truth is that the parts of the world that have contributed the least to climate change are being affected the most. Some of the poorest countries, like Malawi, Mozambique, and Haiti, are the most vulnerable to extreme heat waves, droughts, strong storms, and flooding. And in poorer countries, homes are more easily damaged by storms and floods, and people have fewer resources to adapt to the changes.

A dried-up farm dam near Durbanville, South Africa
John Wilkinson Photography/Moment/Getty Images

That's What We Know.
Here's What We Don't Know:

We don't know how much we'll be able to cut greenhouse gases, so we don't know how much hotter our planet will get, how quickly the ocean will rise, or how many more storms and droughts and wildfires will occur. We don't know the details of how different regions will be affected by climate change.

What Is Being Done?

The good news is that there are lots of smart people working really hard on this problem. Energy that comes from the sun and wind is replacing energy that relies on fossil fuels. This is called **renewable energy**. More people are driving **electric vehicles** instead of gas-powered cars. Cities are being redesigned to adapt to rising seas. Engineers are working on creative solutions to get greenhouse gases out of the atmosphere. Conservancy groups are planting trees and protecting wetlands and forests and coastlines.

Remember Greensburg, the town that was destroyed by a monster tornado in 2007? Now rebuilt, a wind farm powers the town so it doesn't rely on burning fossil fuels. Sinks and toilets use less water. Many of the public buildings generate electricity with solar panels, and new homes have LED lights, energy-efficient appliances, and more insulation so they stay warm and use less energy.

Greensburg City Hall with solar panels

City of Greensburg

What Can *You* Do?

DO THIS AT HOME

- Send a letter to your mayor or governor or senator or president asking them to do more on climate change.

- Write a letter to the editor of your school paper.

- Plant a tree or grow vegetables to reduce carbon dioxide in the air.

- Bike. Walk. Carpool.

- Turn off lights and don't turn the AC or heat up too high. Use fans instead of air conditioning as much as possible when it's hot.

- Eat less meat.

- Keep tires filled with air. A car with flat tires uses more gas.

- Help your school set up a composting program to keep food waste out of landfills.

- Explain how climate change works to a friend.

- Take your friends and siblings outside. Teach them to love the outdoors.

- Most important, speak up! Your voice is needed now more than ever.

Final Thoughts

Now that you know about the weather, consider the forces behind it. The next time it rains, imagine the water condensing around a piece of dirt. Think about warm oceans in one part of the world fueling rainfall in another, making the driest desert burst into bloom.

We are so much better prepared now than we were when that hurricane struck Galveston. We have satellites and supercomputers and hurricane hunters who risk their lives to keep people safe.

Still, the weather is weird, and our tools aren't perfect. And there are really big questions still to answer. For example:

- Why do tornadoes form in some thunderstorms and not others?
- How much better can our weather forecasts get?
- How will climate change affect us locally?
- How can we drastically reduce the emission of greenhouse gases?
- How can we best care for our planet so the weather doesn't keep getting worse?

What we need now are kids like you who appreciate weather's beauty and understand its power. Because these are the kids who will grow up to become meteorologists and climate scientists who study weather to keep people safe. These are the kids who will speak up, who will teach others, and who will work tirelessly to protect our planet.

Can you imagine anything more important than that?

ACKNOWLEDGMENTS

I am indebted to the following scientists and experts who gave their time in interviews and fact-checking:

STACY BARNES, city administrator, Greensburg, Kansas

ALAN EUSTACE, engineer and former senior vice president of engineering, Google

JORDAN GERTH, meteorologist, National Weather Service

ADAM HOUSTON, meteorologist, Professor of Earth and Atmospheric Sciences, University of Nebraska-Lincoln

DAVID JACKSON, Associate Professor, Department of Mathematics, Science, and Social Studies Education, University of Georgia

PETER JACOBS, climate scientist and strategic science advisor for Earth Science in the Office of Communications, NASA Goddard Space Flight Center

JON MEYER, meteorologist and climate scientist, Utah Climate Center, Utah State University

MASTER SERGEANT KAREN P. MOORE, Loadmaster/Dropsonde Operator, 53rd Weather Reconnaissance Squadron, Keesler Air Force Base

BIBLIOGRAPHY AND RESOURCES

Blum, Andrew. *The Weather Machine: A Journey Inside the Forecast*. HarperCollins Publishers: New York, 2019.

Buis, Alan. "Earth's Atmosphere: A Multi-Layered Cake." **NASA Global Climate Change**. October 2, 2019. https://climate.nasa.gov/news/2919/earths-atmosphere-a-multi-layered-cake/.

Carlowicz, Mike, and Stephanie Schollaert Uz. "El Niño." **NASA Earth Observatory**. February 14, 2017. https://earthobservatory.nasa.gov/features/ElNino.

Chang, Kenneth. "Snowflakes as you've never seen them before." *New York Times*. March 10, 2021. https://www.nytimes.com/2021/03/10/science/snowflakes-photos-nathan-myhrvold.html.

"Climate basics for kids." **Center for Climate and Energy Solutions**. https://www.c2es.org/content/climate-basics-for-kids/#.

Fradin, Judith Bloom, and Dennis Brindell Fradin. *Tornado: The Story Behind These Twisting, Turning, Spinning, and Spiraling Storms*. Washington, DC: National Geographic Children's Books, 2011.

"Global Warming vs. Climate Change." **NASA's Global Climate Change**. Last modified November 22, 2022. https://climate.nasa.gov/global-warming-vs-climate-change/.

"Greenhouse Gases." **World Meteorological Organization**. https://public.wmo.int/en/our-mandate/focus-areas/environment/greenhouse-gases#.

Grossman, Nathan, dir. *I am Greta*. November 2020. Hulu, Sveriges Television.

"How do tornadoes form?" **NOAA SciJinks**. Last updated May 15, 2023. https://scijinks.gov/tornado/.

Little, Becky. "How the Galveston Hurricane of 1900 became the Deadliest US Natural Disaster." **History, A&E Television Networks**. Last updated April 12, 2019. https://www.history.com/news/how-the-galveston-hurricane-of-1900-became-the-deadliest-u-s-natural-disaster.

Marder, Jenny. "The World According to Weather Satellites." **NOAA/NASA/ ArcGIS Online**. April 1, 2020. https://storymaps.arcgis.com/stories/3ed 6b70ffa80447aac3fcb1d3378884a.

NASA Climate Kids. Earth Science Communications Team at NASA's Jet Propulsion Laboratory/California Institute of Technology. https:// climatekids.nasa.gov/.

"National Weather Service Safety Tips," **US Dept. of Commerce, NOAA, NWS**. https://www.weather.gov/safety/.

"Raindrops are different sizes." **USGS Water Science School**. June 6, 2018. https://www.usgs.gov/special-topics/water-science-school/science/ raindrops-are-different-sizes.

SkySci for Kids. UCAR Center for Science Education. https://scied.ucar.edu/kids.

"Storm Stories: Greensburg Tornado." **Weather Channel**. July 2, 2019. YouTube video, 5.44. https://www.youtube.com/watch?v=OTfHJZrmXI4.

Thunberg, Greta. "Our House is On Fire." *Fridays for Future*. January 15, 2019. YouTube video. https://www.youtube.com/watch?v=t3dtXewdDSg.

"Water Facts of Life." **US Environmental Protection Agency**. Last modified February 23, 2016. https://www3.epa.gov/safewater/ kids/waterfactsoflife.html.

"What Are Trade Winds?" **NOAA SciJinks**. Last updated May 15, 2023. https://scijinks.gov/trade-winds/.

"What Is the Difference Between Sleet, Freezing Rain, and Snow?" **US Dept. of Commerce, NOAA, NWS**. Last modified December 8, 2013. https://www.weather.gov/iwx/sleetvsfreezingrain.